MW01298306

WHAT'S SO FUNNY ABOUT DEMENTIA?

Pam Mullarkey Robbins, Ph.D.

WESTBOW
P R E S S®
A DIVISION OF THOMAS NELSON
& ZONDERVAN

Copyright © 2021 Pam Mullarkey Robbins, Ph.D.

All rights reserved. No part of this book may be used or reproduced by
any means, graphic, electronic, or mechanical, including photocopying,
recording, taping or by any information storage retrieval system
without the written permission of the author except in the case of
brief quotations embodied in critical articles and reviews.

This book is a work of non-fiction. Unless otherwise noted, the author
and the publisher make no explicit guarantees as to the accuracy of
the information contained in this book and in some cases, names
of people and places have been altered to protect their privacy.

WestBow Press books may be ordered through booksellers or by contacting:

WestBow Press
A Division of Thomas Nelson & Zondervan
1663 Liberty Drive
Bloomington, IN 47403
www.westbowpress.com
844-714-3454

Because of the dynamic nature of the Internet, any web addresses or
links contained in this book may have changed since publication and may
no longer be valid. The views expressed in this work are solely those
of the author and do not necessarily reflect the views of the publisher,
and the publisher hereby disclaims any responsibility for them.

Any people depicted in stock imagery provided by Getty Images are
models, and such images are being used for illustrative purposes only.
Certain stock imagery © Getty Images.

Scriptures taken from the Holy Bible, New International Version®, NIV®.
Copyright © 1973, 1978, 1984, 2011 by Biblica, Inc.™ Used by permission
of Zondervan. All rights reserved worldwide. www.zondervan.com
The "NIV" and "New International Version" are trademarks registered
in the United States Patent and Trademark Office by Biblica, Inc.®

ISBN: 978-1-6642-3719-3 (sc)
ISBN: 978-1-6642-3718-6 (hc)
ISBN: 978-1-6642-3720-9 (e)

Library of Congress Control Number: 2021911914

Print information available on the last page.

WestBow Press rev. date: 9/28/2021

CONTENTS

INTRODUCTION

Written by Pam Mullarkey Robbins, Ph.D.

FACTS ABOUT THIS DISEASE

1. More Than Six Million Americans Are Living With Alzheimer's.
2. Alzheimer's Disease Is The Sixth Leading Cause Of Death In The United States.
3. One In Three Seniors Dies With Alzheimer's Or Another Form Of Dementia-Related Disease.
4. In 2020, Alzheimer's/Other Dementias Cost The Nation $305 Billion.
5. Common Behavioral Symptoms Of Alzheimer's Include Sleeplessness, Wandering, Agitation, Anxiety, And Aggression.

(Fact Sheet, National Institute on Aging, 2019)

PURPOSE IN WRITING THIS BOOK

I found to survive being a caregiver for someone with dementia, it helps to acquire a wonderful sense of humor. Every single day we might cry, get angry, or become frustrated, as we continually repeat answers to their same questions. These emotions are all very normal for caregivers and family members. To survive helping someone with this disease, I suggest trying to find nuggets of humor hidden behind the veil of exhaustion and fear that overwhelm us. Watching the person you know and love start to disappear can be frightening. Not knowing what you can do to stop this disease causes tremendous stress and worry. Sleepless nights are a part of this job, yet sleep is what we need most to be able to deal with our everyday challenges and emotions. Hiding this disease from others is what we usually try to do, yet this is when we need other people's help the most. Not knowing when to let other people know your loved one has dementia can cause us to isolate ourselves, even from our own family members. We think we are trying to protect the person with the disease, but actually, others probably already know something is wrong.

What I am about to suggest will take a change of mind and discipline to accomplish, but if you can try to see the humor in what you are dealing with, your stress level can be reduced. The alternative is daily anxiety, anger and often feelings of depression and loneliness.

Remember life really is short! Research has shown that people who laugh each and every day live 10 years longer than people who don't. So, let's get ready to live longer through laughter!

I am sharing with you some great true stories of the funniest things people say and do when they have dementia. I will share some of my mother's tales. Her name was Lois Hiller Allen, and she was my very best friend all my life. I believe she was the sweetest woman on Earth. She would always tell me how much she loved me and she believed in me. She was my main support person. I could tell her anything whenever I needed to talk. She never judged me. Instead, she would make me solve my own problems through using critical thinking skills. She knew I was very determined and had a strong personality. For me, nothing was impossible and I loved challenges. My mother, on the other hand, liked to be in the background helping my brother and me. Knowing my personality type, she would ask me, "What do you think would happen if..." I would then try to solve the problem with her guidance, yet she actually helped me think I had done it on my own. To this day, I thrive on solving problems. Dementia is one of the biggest problems people around the world are trying to solve. I am not a researcher, but I am a survivor. I have learned one of the greatest secrets to overcoming this emotional and physical rollercoaster is finding humor and sharing your stories with others. Because of my mother's influence, I became a teacher, coach and counselor and hope the stories I share will help you. Please know that you will get through this stressful season with the help of God and others.

My mother loved people and loved to laugh. I trust she would not mind me sharing her stories with you. In fact, I believe she is probably laughing in heaven and hoping her stories will help you find some humor as well.

If you would like to help me write a sequel to this book, please send me your humorous stories that I can share with others. I will not use your name, unless given permission. Together, we can create books that will lift others' spirits and make life a little bit easier for caregivers. So, let's learn how we can deal with dementia by finding the humor in our situations and the situations others are going through. After all, we have no control over the problems we will face, but we do have control over how we will respond to those problems and how we will interact with our loved ones.

Three suggestions I feel I must share.

1. Get enough sleep tonight to be able to face tomorrow. Sleeping pills or natural herbs might be given to the one who is memory-challenged so you can relax knowing that person is asleep. If you need sleep enhancers yourself, talk to your doctor about taking them so you can get the rest you desperately need.
2. Try your best to eat healthy. Eliminate or reduce processed foods and sugars in your

diet. They zap your energy and make you sleepy. Buy fresh vegetables and fruits, and eat beans, nuts and meats to give yourself the vitamins and energy you need. Your diet can dictate your moods. Eat healthy so you are happier and more capable of dealing with the everyday problems you will face. Taking vitamins and supplements can help you stay healthy and avoid sicknesses.

3. Exercise, especially during sundown times each day. If you can take a walk with your memory-challenged person, the endorphins in both of your brains will make you both feel more positive. Sundown is the worst time of day for someone with dementia. If you can get into the habit of exercising before he/she gets moody, you will probably have a less stressed day.

INTRODUCING MY MOM PRIOR TO ALZHEIMER'S

My mom was born to William (Billy) and Daisy Hiller on April 11, 1917, in Concord, New Hampshire. Her parents were in their 40s when they found out Daisy was pregnant. What a shock this was because the local doctors had told Billy and Daisy that she was incapable of bearing children. Prior to her unanticipated pregnancy, Daisy opened up a very successful millinery company that designed beautiful hats for both men and women. Hats were very popular during that era, and most people did not leave home without their hats on their heads. Daisy's shop kept her busy while Billy was working hard to sell more insurance at his own insurance company, named W.W. Hiller Insurance.

Shortly after the birth of my mother, named Lois, her mother, Daisy, became very depressed. Now we have a name for that: postpartum depression. Unfortunately, she never fully recovered from the depression, and she was hospitalized regularly. While in the New Hampshire State Hospital, she received shock treatments, which helped her enough to be able to return home for short periods of time. Unfortunately, the depression always returned, causing her to return to the hospital. There were no medications for depression, as we have today.

My mother, Lois, was never close to her mother but had a wonderful relationship with her father. Her mother was extremely critical of everything my mom did. If Mom brought home five A's and one B, all Daisy would focus on was the B. She would criticize and punish my mother for being such a failure. The verbal abuse was so bad that Mom looked forward to her mother going back to the hospital, so she could live in a peaceful home with her father.

My mother loved horses, so her father made sure she had riding lessons and plenty of time to be at the stables. When she was at the stables, Mom talked to the horses and told them all of her problems while hugging their necks and crying like a baby. She had no one else to tell them to, not even her father, because she didn't want to worry him. Mom was so good at riding horses that she started riding on the circuit, which means she traveled throughout New England competing in horse shows. She won many ribbons, which made her feel successful, in spite of what her mother would tell her.

Mom's favorite five-gated show horse was named Sweet Genius and stood 17 hands high.

In order to compete on the collegiate level, she attended Colby Jr. College in New Hampshire, where she was a member of the equestrian team. She also was a very good athlete and enjoyed snow skiing, ice skating, sledding, swimming and hiking through the woods and mountains in New Hampshire.

My mom met my father, David Allen, at MIT where they were both working. He was tall, dark and handsome, and she fell madly in love with him. Two years after they got married, she gave birth to my older brother, Peter. Two years after his birth, I was born. Five years after that, my baby brother, David, was born. Unfortunately, prior to his first birthday, he died of sudden infant death syndrome.

Lois Allen with her two young babies, Peter and Pam

My mother was very loving to all of us, because she never wanted to be like her abusive mom. She was not a disciplinarian, and my older brother and I took full advantage of that fact. My father traveled every week on work-related business with the Coca-Cola Company. When he was home, he would talk down to my mother. My mother, who endured years of verbal abuse from her own mother, allowed my father to verbally abuse her as well. These rifts caused many fights in our home. As I witnessed her tears after each quarrel, I tried to console her and make her feel loved.

In spite of the verbal abuse, she stayed very active. She was our homeroom mother, she entertained business clients for my dad, and she cooked homemade meals three times a day for her family.

Mom was always fearful that she might become mentally ill like her mother. To overcome that fear, she found many hobbies to keep herself busy and her mind sharp. She was a wonderful tailor and made all of our clothes until we became teenagers and had to have the latest styles. She was a voracious reader, consuming at least one book a week and often up to five.

When we moved to Atlanta, Georgia, Mom became an excellent horseback-riding instructor. I would spend every Saturday at the stables with her, and I eventually became an instructor as well. When I was a teenager, my mother was everyone's favorite mom. All my friends would come to our house, talk to my mom, and tell her all of their problems. Mom would always help anyone who needed it. Each teenager would leave our house feeling so much better and encouraged by her words of affirmation. I never wanted to disappoint my mom because she was my best friend. When other students were making poor choices, I would not join in because I wanted to please my mom.

Mom was great with teenagers, even her own, Peter, 17, and Pam, 15.

After high school graduation, I left Atlanta to attend Jacksonville University in Florida. That is when I really missed my mom more than ever. She was my accountability partner, and I did not have her there with me to help me make decisions in college. There were no cellphones, and I was only permitted to call home on Sundays. That left me on my own, Monday through Saturday, trying to make the right choices. I did not know how to study, and the dorms were very noisy so it was difficult to focus. Of course, there were plenty of parties I wanted to attend as well. I almost failed out of college my first semester, because I was not prepared with the life skills to succeed. Eventually I learned how to say "no," set boundaries, use refusal skills and write written goals. During my four years of college, I became a cheerleader, president of my sorority and secretary of the Student Government Association (SGA). I loved college and learned so many life lessons; many of those lessons were a product of my failures. In spite of my shortcomings, my mother never let me down or criticized me.

In 1969, I married my college cheerleading partner, David Mullarkey. Since I was still in school getting ready to graduate, my mom planned the entire wedding that took place in my hometown of Atlanta, Georgia. We lived in Jacksonville, Florida, after getting married. Mom and Dad loved my husband, David, but missed their daughter being so far away living in Florida. We always spent our holidays together, and my dad and mom told me they were going to eventually move to Jacksonville to be nearer to me.

Christmas in 1970, was celebrated in Jacksonville, Florida with my parents who came to visit from Atlanta, Georgia.

After 33 years of working with the Coca-Cola Company, my dad retired and my parents moved to Jacksonville, Florida, to be near me. When David and I started having children, my mom and dad would always help us. Mom was especially wonderful with the children; she would keep them two mornings a week, so I could play tennis and have time for myself.

My mother was holding Justin, our youngest son, when he was 6 weeks old. She loved her grandsons, and they called her Nanny.

Mom and Dad played tennis twice a week and had such a wonderful retirement. They bought boats and did a lot of traveling on the Intracoastal Waterway. They played bridge every week with a group of friends and were quite social. Life was good and everyone was healthy. We were all very blessed.

Mom and Dad celebrated their 50th anniversary at the Ponte Vedra Inn and Club.

RECOGNIZING WHEN SOMEONE HAS THE DISEASE

I lived three miles from my parents in Jacksonville, Florida. They found a house on the waterway where they could dock their sailboat in their back yard and be nearer to me. My husband and I had two sons who loved their grandparents and stayed with them twice a week. This allowed me to play tennis on my local tennis team. My husband worked hard to allow us to live a comfortable lifestyle and let me stay at home to raise the boys. Life was good, very, very good.

One day, I got a phone call from my mom who was coming to my house to pick up her grandsons. When she spoke on the other end of the phone, I knew something was wrong by the tone of her voice. She was very nervous and agitated at the same time. She said, "Pammy, I don't know where I am or where I am going." I was shocked at what she said because she was on her way to pick up her grandchildren, a joyful task that she willingly had done for over two years. I calmly said, "Mom, you are on your way to our house to pick up the boys. What street are you now on?" She said, "I don't know." I asked her to look for a street sign and read it to me. She had a very difficult time finding a street sign to read. She was on the same street she had driven a hundred times before, but suddenly this day she was lost and overwhelmed with fear.

I knew from that phone call that my dad and I were now going to have to deal with a new problem. I also knew I should not let her drive the boys anymore. She was losing her memory, which not only frightened her, but caused her to get very upset, not knowing what to do about it. I told my father what had happened, and he let me know that Mom had been forgetting many things for the past few months. He had not shared this with me because he did not want to upset me. He felt he could handle this on his own. Frankly,

I believe his pride kept him isolated from me, his only other living family member. I think pride can be a troubling trait that keeps us from facing the unknown. With pride, we stop sharing with loved ones, who are the very people that can help us in times of crisis.

My dad and I knew that we needed to find out what was happening to my mother's memory. We made an appointment with a neurologist, who we heard was the best doctor in his field. One afternoon, we took her to her first neurologist's appointment but did not tell Mom why we were going to see a new doctor. While sitting in the crowded waiting room for what seemed to be forever, we found out people with this disease become easily agitated when having to wait. My mom was no exception. As we sat there with a room full of people who were all waiting for their appointments, she started to fidget in her seat and let out some big sighs of impatience so the nurses could hear her.

After an hour had elapsed, all of a sudden, the office door opened and in walked a very over-weight woman. To everyone's surprise, she was wearing hot pink spandex pants plastered with large purple flowers. As if that was not enough, she had on a purple halter-top with big pink flowers on it. It was quite a sight to see! All Mother needed was to take one look at her, and in her loudest voice, she asked, "Why would anyone that fat wear that tight of an outfit!" Every eye in the waiting room looked at us in shock. My dad and I were mortified beyond words! We were both looking for chairs to crawl under so we could hide. We wanted everyone to know this rude woman was certainly not with us! The good news was the nurses behind the glass heard my mother's outburst about the overweight woman. They quickly decided my mom would need to go into the back to see the doctor before a fistfight broke out in their waiting room.

When the doctor finally arrived in the small examining room where Dad, my mom and I were sitting, he greeted my mother with a smile and a handshake. My agitated mother tried to eke out a smile and pretend she was a sweet Southern belle with the patience of Job. He then asked her, "Well, Mrs. Allen, why did you come here today to see me?" She looked him straight in the eyes and answered, "Well, if you don't know, then why in the world am I here?" At that moment, he realized what he was dealing with, and a long drawn out evaluation probably was not necessary that afternoon. He had a new patient, Lois Hiller Allen, who was not only memory-challenged but also highly agitated.

LESSONS LEARNED:

1. When a person has this disease, even the sweetest of people can become like two-year-olds, having no filter for what they think or say. They say whatever is on their mind, regardless of how rude or caustic it may sound to others.
2. Memory-challenged people become agitated very easily, especially if they have to wait for any length of time.

UNDERSTANDING THE COMBATIVE STAGE

Before Mom's disease affected her brain, she was the sweetest, gentlest person on the face of the Earth. Soon after her diagnosis, she slipped into a six-month combative stage. She was losing her mind and becoming delusional. When she first entered that phase of her disease, she started to turn on me, her best friend. It seemed like she did not remember who I was anymore. She was imagining that I was someone I was not. She was suddenly convinced that I was my father's girlfriend. My dad and I had a good relationship throughout my mom's disease, but believe me, he would never have been my choice for a boyfriend! One day when I knocked on the door of their house, Mom answered the door. Instead of saying "Hello darling, come on in," she looked at me, up one side and down the other. She had a weird look on her face, and I did not know what was going on in her mind. After looking me over and trying to figure out who I was, she exclaimed, "I know who you are. You are my husband's girlfriend, and you can never come back into my house again!" With that, she slammed the door, and no amount of knocking could change her mind.

This was the hardest stage for me to face because she was my best friend, yet she did not even recognize her own daughter. That first day she didn't know who I was, I left their house and cried all the way home. My mind was racing with questions. I wondered how long this delusional state of mind would last. I called my father and shared with him what she had said. He was appalled that she would think I was his girlfriend.

This went on for several weeks, so I did not get to visit in their home, for what seemed to be an eternity. My dad and I talked every day, but Mom would not even come to the phone to talk to me. The entire time my dad and I were talking on the phone, Mom was very irritated and demanded his undivided attention at all times. She was jealous of her own daughter.

One day I had a great idea. I decided to bring over an 8" X 10" picture of myself from my college graduation. I knew if she saw that picture and then saw me, she would be able to reason that I was truly who I said I was, her only daughter that she dearly loved. As soon as my mom opened the door, I said, "Look at this picture and tell me who you see?" She looked at my picture for quite a long time and then very softly raised her hand and touched the picture of my face through the non-reflective glass. She smiled as she recognized the picture of me. Then she said in a very quiet, sad voice, "Oh, that's my daughter, Pammy. I love her so much, but she never comes to see me anymore." With that recognition, I said, "Mom, look at the picture and now look at me. See I am your daughter, Pammy, your best friend and the one who loves you the most." She then looked at the picture and then back at me. Abruptly she said, "I know who you are little lady. You cannot fool me. You are my husband's girlfriend! Now get out of here before I beat you up!" Once again, the door slammed in my face, and I cried all the way home, realizing that I had lost my best friend and confidant. I missed her so very much. I realized I could no longer rely on her for help. She would now need to rely on me for help. I could no longer ask her for advice in raising our two young sons. I could never again call her to tell her about my day and hear her calming voice that would always make me feel better. The roles were now reversed, and I would never be her little daughter again. At that moment, I did not know and really did not want to know what was in store for our futures. I just knew I missed my mother and wanted her back again. It was almost like experiencing a death in the family. The person I once relied upon had vacated her body.

LESSONS LEARNED:

1. The combative stage lasts longer than we want and there is very little anyone can do to restore or change a person's mind. Delusions of persecution can be a very

trying part of this disease. Agreeing with the person is much easier than trying to make sense of what she is saying. Attempting to talk a person out of their delusion does not work. That only causes more agitation and frustration for both people.

2. Changing the person's surroundings can help. I found out during that six-month combative stage, that getting my mom away from her home and bringing her to my house to visit allowed her to see me as her daughter and not as my dad's girlfriend. During this time, my favorite expression was, "This too shall pass." At the end of six months of visiting at my house, my mother once again allowed me into her own home. Thankfully, she never again accused me of being my father's girlfriend. The combative stage was over, and a new phase was getting ready to start.

3. Personalities may change. Unfortunately, there is nothing we can do to prevent that from happening. The person we once knew and loved eventually leaves us and

becomes a new, very confused person. This new individual needs unconditional love, reassurance and a lot of encouragement, the very things the caregiver needs as well.

PLAYING GAMES CAN HELP YOU GET COOPERATION

Since this disease affects the mind, the person becomes more like a child. I found that games work wonders when we need the person's cooperation. My mother was scared to death to have water put on her face, yet she needed to keep up her hygiene. Dad could not get her into the shower at home, so one day I asked him to bring her over to our house and I would care for her and get her to bathe. This would also give my dad an opportunity to have a day for himself, not having to worry about Mom. It was the end of November, and I was decorating the Christmas tree when Mom arrived. I could tell by her odor that she had not had a shower for quite some time. I decided to fix a bath in my large tub. I had gone to the nearest Burger King that morning and gotten a paper crown for the game I was about to introduce.

I brought Mom back to the bathroom and with the excitement of a game show host, I told her we were going to play *Queen for a Day*! This was one of her favorite shows in prior years. When I was just a child, we would watch it on TV. There were three women contestants who all told their life stories. The saddest story would then win the prize of becoming *Queen for a Day.* The winner of the contest received a golden crown to wear along with many gifts.

My mom remembered the show, and she could hardly wait to play. I told her that if she would get into the tub and allow me to bathe her, she would win and become *Queen for a Day*! Her grand prize would be to choose one of the three perfumes I had sitting on the counter. She then allowed me to help undress her, get her into the tub, bathe her and help her out of the tub before dressing her. She then chose one of the perfumes and dabbed it on her neck. Happily, she picked up the paper crown and proudly wore it on her head all day long. *Queen for a Day* became our favorite game from then on. She never tired of playing it. This was the only way we could get her to take a bath.

Burger King's employees loved seeing me come in for a breakfast sandwich, since they knew I would wear their crown out of the restaurant and give it to my mother when she would come to visit.

LESSONS LEARNED:

1. Make things fun. Remind memory-challenged people of their prior experiences. Bring up forgotten stories, games and songs they once loved. They might not know anything about today, but they readily recall old memories. They can even remember the words to former songs they once loved.
2. Remember bribery works every time, so make it fun, enjoyable and give them a prize to help keep them motivated.
3. Because their minds become child-like, be patient, talk to them very slowly and with great compassion.
4. You may have to repeat yourself over and over again. Do not try to understand it; just do it and it will make your life a lot easier.

They do not remember what they just asked you or what your answer was, so keep repeating and know this is a very frustrating part of the disease for both of you.

I went to the local Burger King to get my mother a crown to wear so she could be Queen for a Day.

The only way we could get Mom to take a bath was to play Queen for a Day, which was one of her favorite TV shows in the 50s.

DISCOVERING GAMES SOMETIMES DON'T WORK

The day before Christmas, my dad dropped off my mom at our house. Mom and I were going to have some fun putting on the last of the tree decorations and starting to prepare for the big Christmas meal. I have always loved this holiday because, in our home, Christmas represented Jesus coming to Earth as a baby and showing what God's love is truly like. Our family always celebrated the holiday, and gift-giving was always the best part.

That day, I had wonderful plans to be alone with my mom, just as we used to be before she got dementia. We wanted to cook, be together, laugh and just have fun. It was going to be a wonderful time for just Mom and me.

The boys were in the back yard playing war games with their friends. They would all dress up in camo, take their toy rifles, get into the canoe and travel down the drainage ditches to fight their battles. They had built forts on vacant property and had some wonderful wars. As most boys do, they all had a blast every day while on Christmas vacation. My dad and my husband went off to run errands and spend time at the hardware store, doing whatever men enjoy doing at those kinds of places. My dad really needed a break from mother's constant caregiving. He and my husband were good friends, so Dad could pour out his heart to him.

When Mom arrived, it was obvious that she had refused to take a bath for several days. By this time, she had become so stubborn that my dad just gave up on the idea of bathing her. I knew I could help her take a bath and smell clean so she could be ready for Christmas day. I said in my enthusiastic voice, "Hey Mom, before we trim the rest of the tree, let's play Queen for a Day, okay?" She looked at me with a look that could kill and said, "NO!" She was not a happy camper, and I did not realize how agitated she was. After I asked her for the 10th time to play our little game, she said to me, "If you don't stop talking to me about taking a bath, I am going to run away!" A little later, I thought I would try it just one more time. When I mentioned bathing, to my shock, she went right out the front door and started walking down the street all by herself. Thank God, she was fully dressed, but unfortunately, she was running away. I was shocked that she really did what she threatened to do. I knew her health was not good enough to allow her to walk very far. I decided to walk about 50 feet behind her so she would not get lost. What I did not realize was when people with dementia get highly agitated, they regain the strength they once had as teenagers!

She kept walking at a rather good clip for someone her age. I followed about 50 feet behind her the entire time, hoping she would wear herself out and want to go back to my house. As she rounded the third block, I thought to myself, surely, she is getting ready to turn around. Wrong! She kept walking. She occasionally looked back at me and saw that I was following her. I thought this would make her feel secure, but again I was wrong. It made her even more agitated that someone was following her. She eventually turned around and said to me in her loudest voice, "If you don't stop following me, I am going to beat you up!" I was in total shock at what she had just said, but I knew I had to follow her because she would not remember how to get back to our house.

The next time she turned around, there I was still following her. Now, she had had it with me. In her fury, she quickly walked up to me, balled up her fist and punched me right in the nose! I was so surprised that my best friend and mother had just tried to punch my lights out. That is when I reached up and held her arms. I hoped that would keep her from hitting me anymore. She kept trying to pull her arms away, but I would not let go of her. That made her super furious!

To my surprise, a concerned neighbor was watching this sight from her window, and she called the police. Within a minute or two, a police car drove up to where my mom and I were standing in the middle of the street, the very site of the first fistfight I had ever had!

Having a policeman bring Mom back to my house was one of the most embarrassing moments of my life!

As soon as my mom caught a glimpse of the police car, she ran over and screamed in her loudest voice, "HELP ME, OFFICER, HELP ME! She then continued to tell him, "This woman has been trying to poison me for the last three months!" Oh no! I could not believe the words that had just come out of her mouth! I was in complete shock and did not know what to do or say. As I looked at my mother standing next to the police officer's car, my mind was racing with thoughts about how hard I had tried to help her through this disease. After all, I had put a lot of my life on hold to be there for her every day. I had never hurt her in any way, nor had I ever wanted to do her any harm. Now she was telling the authorities that I was trying to poison her.

The officer got out of his patrol car and asked me my name and address. When I gave it to him, he recognized it and said, "Aren't you my school board representative?" I sheepishly said, "Yes, officer, and this is my mother, Mrs. Allen, who has Alzheimer's disease." He looked at me and said, "I can't believe my very own school board member is trying to poison her own mother!" He then commanded, "Get in the car Mrs. Allen, and I will take you home." I gave him the address to our house. As he drove off with my mother in his police car, I began what seemed to be the longest walk of my life to get back to my home. I was very humiliated and wanted to crawl into a hole. I thought for sure my reputation as an elected official was now going to be totally destroyed.

When I finally got back to my street, I noticed the police officer was standing outside of his patrol car waiting for me to get there. My mother was still in the front passenger's seat of his car. He asked me quite impatiently, "How do I get her out of my car?" I had to hold back my first reaction, which was to laugh my head off. Containing myself, I asked him, "What is the problem officer?" He said,

"She won't get out of the car until her husband comes to get her, and I need to go to another call."

Since cellphones were not yet invented, I could not call my father for help. I told the officer to wait a minute and let me see if my son and his friends were in the house and could help get her out of his patrol car. I ran into the house where my 10-year-old son, Justin, and his five friends, dressed in their usual camouflage, were at the kitchen table eating cookies and drinking milk. They had been fighting wars and having the time of their lives. One look at me and they sensed by my demeanor that something was very wrong. A thought immediately came to my mind that I could bribe them with money to help me. I said, "If you strong guys can get Nanny out of the nice policeman's squad car, I will give each of you $5." They looked at each other and, with the confidence of Olympic wrestlers, said, "Sure we will have her out in a jiffy. Be right back!" As the kitchen door closed, I wondered how easily it would be for them to get her out when she was so agitated. I did not have the courage nor the energy to go outside to watch.

Within 10 minutes, the boys came back into the kitchen. I looked up from the table, and to my surprise, I saw that their hair was all messed up, and a couple of them had big holes in their camo shirts. They looked at me and said, "You can keep your $5!" My son then said, "Mom, don't ever ask me to do something like that again!" They immediately picked up their toy rifles, ran out the back door, got into the camouflaged flat bottom canoe and paddled off as fast as they could to get away from our house. This was their first real and biggest battle they had ever fought!

After that idea failed, I decided to call my friend and neighbor, Emily Campbell. She was a registered nurse and knew how to deal with elderly, agitated patients. Her father had died of the same horrible disease that my mother was suffering from, so she knew exactly what to do. She reassured me that she would be right over. I thanked God as I held back the tears that were starting to form in my eyes. I then prayed and cried out to God, "Please help me."

To my great surprise, God answered my prayer almost immediately. Just as I closed the front door on my way out to the police car, my dad and husband drove into the driveway. They were finally back from the hardware store. They had a wonderful time together. The two of them were smiling, looking all rested and feeling relaxed. What a relief it was for me to see them pull into the driveway!

My mom took one look at my dad, opened the police car door, jumped out, ran, and got into my father's car. The police officer not only looked shocked but very relieved as he got into his patrol car and drove off to his waiting call. Thank God, he did not give me a ticket, but I realized he forgot to say goodbye. I am sure the story he told back at the police station was a doozy.

As my dad got out of his car, I started to tell him in a calm, quiet voice what had happened. I did not want his day to be ruined, so I told him the short version and skip all the sordid details. While I was telling him what had happened, my friend Emily, the RN, drove up and parked behind my dad's car. My mother was sitting in the passenger's seat of my dad's car and happened to look behind her. When she saw beautiful, blonde Emily talking to my dad, she became delusional and thought Emily must be my dad's girlfriend.

My father was a very faithful man. He never cheated on my mother, but in my mother's mind, he was cheating and that is all that mattered to her. Mom became very angry at this imaginary new affair that she thought her husband was having. In her fury, she decided to close the windows in the car and lock all the doors. Then she proceeded to lay her hand on the horn. We could not get into the locked car, and she was not going to stop honking the horn or get out of the car. By that time, I am sure the neighbors were all looking out their windows wondering what in the world was happening at their school board member's house.

Emily and I decided to go into the kitchen, so she could dissolve a tranquilizer into a glass of water. I asked Emily to stay in the kitchen to prevent my mom from getting more upset. I brought out the glass of water to my dad, and he showed it to Mom through the passenger side window. My mom was very hot with the windows rolled up. Living in Florida makes it quite steamy, especially in a car with no open windows for ventilation. Seeing the glass of water convinced Mom to unlock the doors of the car. She drank the entire glass, pill and all, in one big gulp!

My dad could see that I was an emotional wreck, so he said goodbye and drove her home. When she arrived home, she went inside, got into her bed and slept for over 18 hours!

The beauty of this disease is that sick people do not have any recollection of the things that happened in the immediate past. They can remember things from years ago, but recent memories get erased. How I wished we caregivers had the ability to do that too.

LESSONS LEARNED:

1. There will be embarrassing moments in our lives that will truly humble us in ways no other thing can do. When that happens, it is okay. Go ahead; you have permission to get alone, to cry, to get angry and to throw a royal fit. I promise you will feel better afterwards!

2. The person with dementia will not have any recollection of recent events or things they

have said or done. Try to forgive and forget, so you can carry on and not let bitterness form inside of your soul.

3. Keeping your emotions healthy is a challenge for sure, but unforgiveness will rob you of your strength and joy. Forgive immediately even though you do not feel like it. Remember, forgiveness is a choice not a feeling. It frees you, keeps your soul healthy and allows you to see things through fresh eyes.

4. Ask God to help you through every challenge. He hears your prayers and knows how you are suffering. He will calm you. He will never leave you, nor forsake you. He will help you get through this, and you will come out the other side a victor, not a victim. You will be an overcomer not be overcome.

GETTING DIRTY
IS PROBABLY
UNAVOIDABLE!

I wanted to give my father a break and help my mother feel loved and special, so I took her to the elegant Alhambra Dinner Theater in Jacksonville, Florida, where we lived. Mom and I both dressed up in our finest outfits. We looked like a million bucks, if I do say so myself. We looked into the mirror, smiled with delight and admired ourselves. She wore the beaded long gown that she had worn to my wedding years prior. I wore a brand new full-length white suit I had bought the day before. I must say, we were in all of our glory!

The dinner was delicious, and the play was very entertaining. Mom and I were really enjoying our time together, and she even laughed at the humorous parts of the play. It seemed like old times, just my mom and me together without having to worry about a thing. What a wonderful gift we were both enjoying.

About 10 minutes before the intermission break, I told Mom we needed to go to the restroom, so we could avoid the crowds. She got up and followed me into the powder room where there were only three stalls. She went into one stall and locked the door. I went into the one next to her and locked my door. The problem started when we both finished, but only one of us reappeared. Mom was stuck in her stall, and she could not figure out how to unlock the door. This was not rocket science! It was a simple lock. You just had to slide it to unlock it. I tried for 10 minutes to get her to follow my directions: "Mom, take the silver knob and slide it to the right." She was too confused to be able to do it. Fortunately, the bathroom stall had a 12- to 18-inch opening at the bottom. Unfortunately, the floors were very old and quite dirty. I tried to negotiate with her once more, but she could not figure out how to slide the knob to unlock her door. By now, she was getting very upset. Agitation was rearing its ugly head, yet once again.

Then the intermission started. I knew the restroom would fill up with dozens of women who had to go to the bathroom very badly. I knew I had to do something drastic, and there seemed to be no other alternative. That is when I got down on the dirty floor in my new, white, full-length suit and proceeded to do a GI Joe crawl to get under my mother's bathroom stall door.

There was my mom looking very puzzled when she saw me on the floor. She asked me, "Why are you on the floor?" I did not take time to answer her. Instead, I pulled myself up from the floor and easily slid the knob that unlocked the door. As I opened the door, the women who were waiting impatiently in a long line looked at my mom and me in complete wonder. I am sure they were thinking, "Why in the world would both of them be coming out of the same stall?"

It was a tight squeeze with the two of us trying our hardest to get out of a one-person stall at the same time. The women in line were getting frustrated because they really had to go badly. Then a woman, who I am sure was just trying to be helpful, said to me, "Excuse me, but did you know you have dirt all over your white suit?" My first thought was to knock her lights out. Instead, I zipped my lips and burst into tears. I grabbed my mother's hand and left the dinner theater in lightning speed. I figured my mom did not remember what she had seen in the first act and certainly would not remember missing the rest of the play either.

I tried to hide my tears, but they fell from my cheeks as I drove home to her house. After all, this was supposed to have been our elegant evening at the dinner theater. When my dad saw my filthy suit and my red eyes from crying, he did not say a word with the exception of "Thank you. I will call you tomorrow." I went home and cried myself to sleep. I prayed to God, "I don't think I can do this Lord. Please forgive me and help me."

The next day when I saw my father and started to tell him all that had happened at the dinner theater, I began to laugh. Before I could finish the story, the two of us were belly laughing hysterically. Mom was even laughing with us, though she had no idea why she was laughing!

LESSONS LEARNED:

1. My dad and I agreed to focus on the humor of the day instead of the messes we had already experienced. We knew we were probably going to have to experience more of these in the future.

2. Your best plans may blow up, but try not to blow up with them! It is okay to have a meltdown, to cry out to God and allow the Lord to restore you and give you strength for the next day. You will need it.

3. Relish the times you have together that seem normal, because unfortunately they might not last. Try to focus on the good times and not the bad.

4. Don't be angry and become impatient when others do not understand your dilemma. Be thankful that they are not experiencing what you are having to endure.

5. Lower your expectations, and be flexible when things do not go according to what you planned.

The Alhambra Dinner Theater is a wonderful place to watch a live play, enjoy a delicious dinner and be with loved ones.

LOOKING FOR THE RIGHT NURSING HOME

My dad and I knew we had to make a change and get mother into a 24- hour facility where she could be cared for properly. Mom's disease was wearing out my dad. We had to sell her car because she would sneak out and drive. She was a terrible driver before dementia and afterwards she was a 2,000-pound steel wrecking ball!

For some ridiculous reason, the state of Florida sent my mother a five-year extension for her driver's license. When we opened up the letter, Mom was standing next to us and saw her driver's license. Dad and I knew she needed to stop driving. We figured the best way to handle the driving issue was to sell her car and get her keys out of the house. That way she would forget she ever had a car, and our problem would be solved. WRONG!

After we sold her car and it was no longer parked in the garage, she would open the garage door about every hour and scream, "Dave, call the police! Someone has stolen my car." Getting her calmed down was a huge ordeal. Afterwards, she would not remember anything she had said or done. Within 30-60 minutes after settling down, she would once again go to the garage door and scream that her car had been stolen. This went on for weeks.

About that time, my dad was at his wit's end. She would ask him the same question over 100 times a day. He was losing weight and becoming very depressed and short-tempered trying to deal with my mom. We knew we had to find a nursing home where she could get round-the-clock care and my father could get some much-needed rest and find some peace of mind.

We found a daycare that served people with memory loss. They agreed to allow mother to stay for a few hours. This afforded Dad and me an opportunity to look for a nursing home. She had never been away from my father or me since the disease started, almost five years prior. My mom was unsure about getting out of the car once we arrived at the daycare. When we told her there was a hair salon inside where she could get her hair done, she agreed to enter. The caregivers were very sweet and took her over to the salon chair while we were able to slip out the door. We expected she would be fine for a few hours getting her hair done and sitting with the other patrons. We thought she would enjoy being pampered and meet new friends while waiting for our return.

After Dad and I visited several prospective nursing homes, we finally found one that met our expectations. It had white tablecloths, linen napkins and a very pretty dining room, filled with light. Mother loved light shining through windows. While at our selected nursing facility, we had a chance to meet the two owners and felt very comfortable having Mother move there. It was smaller than most other facilities. The staff referred to all the patients as guests. They also addressed each guest as "Mr." or Mrs." followed by their last name. Their staff knew every person's name and treated them with love and respect. Finally, we were starting to see a light at the end of the tunnel and feeling somewhat relieved for the first time in over five years.

When we returned to the daycare to pick up my mother, we noticed a police car with the lights flashing in front of the building. Our hearts sank, knowing the police were probably there because of something Mom had done. Just as we suspected, unfortunately we were right.

After she had her hair done, she told the staff at the daycare she was leaving and going to walk home. The daycare personnel told Mom she would have to wait until her husband and daughter came to get her. That set her off like a rocket; she started screaming she had been abducted! No matter how hard these seasoned staff members tried, they could not calm her down. When we arrived, the staff, the police officers and mother looked like they had all been in a boxing match for the past two hours. As Dad and I apologized profusely, we did our best to make amends. In addition, we generously tipped the staff. Unfortunately, even money did not stop them from asking us to please not bring back Mrs. Allen for another visit. We assured them that we had found a nursing home for her, so they could relax.

LESSONS LEARNED:

1. Change is extremely difficult for people with memory loss and for their family and caregivers as well. The good news for the patients is they do not remember what they have put the caregivers through. The bad news is the caregivers cannot forget the emotional rollercoaster they have had to ride!

2. There may come a time when 24-hour care is essential, not only for the person with the disease but especially for the caregiver.

3. Caregiving is a very hard job, and if the caregiver burns out, the patient will suffer as well. There is nothing wrong with getting help. Getting help is essential for the caregiver's emotional and physical well-being.

4. Family members need to stick together and support the caregivers trying to help them. It is easy to blame others instead of recognizing the need for a break for those caring for the patient.

Southside Nursing Home was the perfect place for my mother. Every staff member knew her name. Family members were always encouraged to join in with the activities that included reading circles, dances, music, singing and church services.

REALIZING THE PERSON'S SPIRIT IS STILL ALIVE AND WELL!

Moving Mom to the Nursing Home

Before my mom got Alzheimer's, I shared with her about Christ coming into my life and the lives of our family members. I shared how He put us back together and how we were now a family full of joy, peace and unity as never before. Mom would always say, "I am happy for you, but I don't need a crutch," or she would say, "I took you to church and am a good person and don't need anything else." By this time, I had given up on helping her asking Christ into her heart. Jesus said, *"Here I am! I stand at the door and knock. If anyone hears my voice and opens the door, I will come in and eat with that person, and they with me."* (Revelation

3:20) Jesus is a gentleman and will never force His way into a person's life. He waits to be invited.

My father had lost 60 pounds, and my mother was wandering around the neighborhood at night. At that point, we both knew my dad could not continue caring for her. We were ready to move Mom into the nursing home we had found. The day before we were going to move her out of her home and into the nursing home, I took her to the beautiful Ponte Vedra Club for lunch. At that time with her disease, she had lost the ability to talk and put words together. She was very quiet, but still smiled a lot.

We had a lovely time at our table, overlooking the ocean below. I shared stories with her about our former years. It was a wonderful lunch filled with good memories and a beautiful afternoon looking out at the ocean.

Most of our best memories were centered around water, whether it was the on the ocean, at the lake, or in a pool. Our entire family loved boating and swimming. We spent our happiest times boating as a family. I shared stories with her about sailing and motor boating. Mom and Dad took a vacation each year on their boat until Mom got dementia. Then it was too stressful for her to make a change from being at home to sleeping on the boat.

Boating was a way of life in my family. I was on a sailboat when I was a young baby, and my parents always had a boat during their lives.

Spending time at the beach and outdoors was what we did as a family for recreation.

I knew changing Mom's environment would cause great stress because of being memory-challenged. I knew consistent surroundings made her feel safe and assured. I felt extremely uneasy and fearful just thinking about moving her from her familiar environment.

As I drove her home from our wonderful lunch, I tried one last time to share with her about how Christ took away all my fears and how He had always been with me, especially during hard times.

As my car reached the top of the bridge over the Intracoastal Waterway, something wonderful and unexpected happened. My mother, who could no longer speak or put words together, said in a clear voice, "I think I would like that too." I was so amazed that she not only spoke, but she also wanted to have Christ come into her life.

I immediately pulled the car over onto the maintenance lane on the top of the bridge. I then took hold of my mother's hands and prayed that Christ would come into her heart and be with her for all eternity. I had tears of joy running down my face. As Mom looked over at me from the passenger's seat, she lifted her wrinkled fingers and gently wiped my tears from my cheeks. I was speechless and so grateful that God had given me that special moment to be with my mother. I now knew that she had the gift of eternal life, and we would be together again someday forever. Only this time would be different. She would have a glorified body and would have the mind of Christ. She would have her memory back and be able to talk with me and share so many wonderful memories we had together. I now knew I could be at peace, because we would be together for all eternity. God's timing is perfect.

After praying with my mom on the top of the bridge, I drove her home. As I walked her up to the front door, I knew this would be the last time she was going to spend the night in her home with my father. Tomorrow, Dad and I would take her to the nursing home. She had no idea what was going to happen and neither did we. My heart was so heavy about her having to leave her home. I knew she would be afraid, and I wanted to carry that fear for her, but was unable to do so. She had to make this difficult transition in order to keep my father alive and healthy. The weight of that was more than I could carry, so I prayed to God to help my dad and me.

As Mom and I approached the front door, she turned around and said the last understandable sentence I would ever hear her say. She looked at me and said, "I think today is going to be a new day." I looked back at her and said, "Yes mother, this is a new day and you are made new. The Bible says, *"Therefore, if anyone is in Christ, the new creation has come: The old has gone, the new is here!"* (2 Corinthians 5:17) I was so amazed that God would show me that everything was going to be okay. He had this, and I no longer had to worry and carry such a heavy burden.

I hugged her goodbye, got back into my car and cried all the way home. I was so grateful God granted my prayer, that my mom would become a believer. It took having full-blown Alzheimer's disease before she accepted Christ. It reminded me of what Jesus said about coming to Him as a child with childlike faith.

LESSONS LEARNED:

1. Never give up on someone's salvation. It might not happen until the very end, but prayers work and God honors our requests for our loved ones. Jesus promised, *"If you remain in me and my words remain in you, ask whatever you wish, and it will be done for you."* (John 15:7)

2. When and if it the time comes to place a loved one in a nursing home, it will be heart-wrenching but necessary in order to keep the caregiver healthy. In addition, compliance with stringent state eldercare regulations may exceed the caregiver's abilities to fulfill.

3. It is important to understand the time when it is necessary to remove the heavy burden from the caregiver. As much as the caregiver desires to be the one caring for the patient, there might come a time when it is evident that the burden is beyond the abilities of family and friends.

4. Whether it means hiring full-time or part-time help at home or moving the patient to

a long-term care facility, the need has to override any guilt one may feel. There is a significant cost to either of those choices, but the cost of a caregiver's life is one of the most important priorities.

5. Neglect can eventually slip in caused by the spiraling decline of care for the patient, whose health is getting worse. When the patient is prone to falling, he/she needs to be kept in either a wheelchair or a hospital bed. That is when the patient may begin to resist being moved, become very heavy to lift and almost impossible to roll over. Changing diapers becomes a tremendous burden. Even feedings become more complicated than they once were.

6. Caregivers often totally lose their independence and start to become depressed, because of having to stay with the patient around the clock. These are normal feelings that often signal outside qualified help should be brought in, or the patient should be placed in an out-of-home facility.

FINDING SPECIAL GUESTS AT THE NURSING HOME

Guest Story #1: Mr. Davis

It was a very difficult day taking my mother to the nursing home for the first time. Dad and I lied to her and said she was going on a short vacation and we would be back soon. She was extremely confused, but the nurses were so kind and made her feel very welcome. The next day, my dad and I drove to the nursing home to see how she had done on her first night away from home.

When we walked in the front door of the facility, we saw Mom in the main lobby sitting in a chair beside an elderly man who was in a wheelchair. His name was Mr. Davis. To our surprise, they were holding hands and smiling at each other. I could tell my dad was getting a bit jealous about what we were seeing. One of the nurses came over and reassured us that Mrs. Allen and Mr. Davis were just friends, even though in their minds, they were convinced they were married to each other. When the nurse left us alone, I said to my dad, "You know, Dad, Mom has never been alone. You have always been there for her, and she cannot be alone without someone to help her. I am sure Mr. Davis can't catch her to do anything romantic." My dad looked straight at me and said, "That is not what I am worried about." I said, "Dad, then why are you worried?" He abruptly answered, "Do you think Mr. Davis would pay half of what this is costing me to have her live here?" My dad was very frugal. He would have loved to have Mr. Davis help pay a portion of her bills!

LESSONS LEARNED:

1. Get ready for major surprises and changes. My mom and Mr. Davis stayed good friends until he died several months after she arrived at the nursing home. Mom always

wanted Dad to take her home with him, but he could not do that. That was the hardest thing either of us had to do: see her clinging to his arm and cry to be able to go home with us. Dad and I would usually be quiet all the way home, neither of us wanting to start to cry and upset the other.

2. Good things come out of even the worst situations. One wonderful thing happened during the seven months of going to the nursing home together. My father and I became good friends. He and I did not have a close relationship until Mom got sick. Then we leaned on each other for support and comfort. I had tried all my life to do enough good things to hear my dad say, "I love you." Because of his upbringing, people did not talk about feelings, especially feelings involving affection. Consequently, he did not tell me he loved me until he was 78 and I was 46 years old. When he was 78, he had received Christ into his heart, and he became a much kinder man. Growing up, I had not known him as anything but strict

and authoritative, yet he was also a good provider. Even though God was working in his heart, he did not want to attend church but read a scripture every day on a flip calendar that I had given him. Through reading a sentence from God's word each day on his calendar, he started to become loving and appreciative. I am so thankful that we became very good friends. That was quite a day when for the first time I heard those wonderful words, "I love you, Pammy."

Guest Story #2: Mrs. Levy

At the nursing home, I was warned by many of the staff to avoid Mrs. Levy at all times. She was another Alzheimer's patient, who was about six feet tall and very strong. From what the staff told me, she was mean and hateful. Mrs. Levy was also known to be dangerous. At times, she would physically hurt people. I knew who she was and tried to avoid her at all costs.

One day, I was sitting in my mother's room on her bed and in walked Mrs. Levy, uninvited! I was in shock and did not know what to do or say. She walked toward me, looking at me with a harsh glare. I figured I was about to get physically hurt. However, unexpectedly, out of my mouth came these words: "Hello, Mrs. Levy. Would you like to sit down on the bed with me and meet my friend Jesus?" She immediately sat down beside me and listened attentively as I shared about Jesus Christ dying for her sins and offering her the free gift of eternal life. When I finished, I ask her, "Mrs. Levy, would you like to invite Jesus Christ into your heart and have His free gift of eternal life, so you can be with God in heaven when you die?" She shook her head "yes," and we held hands and prayed. When the prayer was over, she got up, smiled at me, and walked out of the room. I think she was a changed person from that day on because of God's Holy Spirit was now living inside of her.

LESSONS LEARNED:

1. Although a person's brain may no longer be functioning, every person has a spirit that lives within him or her. God gives each of us a spirit when we are born. I believe we

all have a longing to know God personally. It doesn't matter what age or what kind of physical shape a person is in, the spirit inside is being drawn by God. Eventually, many people will surrender to His calling.

2. The cliché goes, "Do not judge a book by its cover." We can learn so much from that saying when dealing with people. The staff warned me about Mrs. Levy, but I needed to see her as God saw her, needing someone to love her unconditionally and reconcile her back to her creator. She had the same need in her spirit that all of us have. Once we find that, we are truly satisfied and at peace in our hearts.

Guest Story #3: Pastor Roberts

A precious man, I will call Pastor Roberts, had been a preacher for over 50 years. He was at the same nursing home with my mom. He had good days, but he also had very bad days. On his good days, he was the sweetest man of all the guests at the home, always smiling and patting people's hands. I loved talking to him, but on his bad days, he would cuss like a sailor and become very belligerent. His sweet wife and daughter would visit him daily, and we became friends. When he would start cussing, they were mortified! They would apologize to me repeatedly saying, "He never said a cuss word in his life and was a good preacher and a very godly man. We don't know what happened to cause these outbursts and foul mouth!" I would assure them that those words did not offend me. I was beginning to understand the most saintly people on Earth could change on a dime, when suffering with dementia.

LESSON LEARNED:

Dementia can change a person's personality in a split second. Mood swings are excerbated with this disease. A sweet person one day can turn into a hateful person the next day. Remember, the real person you once knew is still there somewhere and experiencing this trauma as well.

Guest Story #4: Mr. Watkins

There was a crusty old man named Mr. Watkins who was in a wheelchair at the nursing home. One day I walked into the open reception area and found him extremely upset. I went right over to him and asked him what I could do to help him. He screamed in his loudest voice, "Nothing! The vampires came last night and sucked out all my blood!"

Having a Ph.D. in counseling did not help one bit when it came to calming him down or getting him stabilized. None of my best-educated efforts worked that day with Mr. Watkins. I tried to convince him to look at the veins in his hands and understand that the bluish lines were veins filled with blood. I told him that he would not be alive without his blood. Whatever I said would not convince him that the vampires did not leave him bloodless.

After 30 minutes and no success, in walked Pastor John Dawson. I had been one of John's teachers at Episcopal High School. He was a funny guy, not only as a teenager in my class, but as an adult as well. I motioned for him to come help me. He immediately came over to Mr. Watkins and asked him what was going on. Mr. Watkins let Pastor John know, without hesitation, that vampires had come into his room last night and sucked out all his blood! Pastor John took one look at Mr. Watkins and said, "I can believe that. Those vampires sucked out all my blood last night too!"

When Pastor John said that, Mr. Watkins smiled at John and exclaimed with excitement, "You too?" Pastor John agreed that he too had no blood left. Mr. Watkins calmed down immediately, was all smiles and had made a new best friend named Pastor John. He then asked Pastor John to wheel him to his room because he was too exhausted to stay awake and needed to take a nap. Actually, I was the one that needed the nap more than he did.

LESSONS LEARNED:

1. Don't ever try to reason with a person with dementia. They can be out of their minds, and we just need to agree with them and reassure them. Agreeing with them saves so much time and energy and keeps them calm. Reasoning does not usually work, so amuse them by just agreeing with their delusions. You will save a lot of energy.

2. When a person suffers with dementia, everyone associated with that family member suffers as well. The primary caregiver has the most difficult time of all. The caregiver wants to keep the person alive, but at the same time, he/she wants that person to pass on, so he/she can have some type of life other than caregiving. Before my mom went to the nursing home, my dad could no longer sail his boat, have coffee with the men friends he had made in the neighborhood, go out to eat at a restaurant, or even read a book because of the constant needs of my mom. I had watched my dad become exhausted, irritable, hopeless and depressed. Putting Mom in a nursing home gave him his first bit of freedom. We went to visit Mom regularly, but he did not have to watch her every minute of every day and night.

3. God does answer prayers. My dad and I were both concerned about the cost of the nursing home, so I started to pray that God would take my mom home so my dad would

still have enough savings to enjoy the rest of his life. God answered my prayer. Within seven months after Mom moved into the nursing home, she died and went to be with the Lord.

FEARING DEATH CAUSED TREMENDOUS ANXIETY

K nowing that mother would soon die and I would have to face that day weighed heavily on my heart and mind. In order for you to understand how terrified I was of death, I am going to share with you my background of having to deal with death as a child and young woman.

When I was five years old, my mother brought home a new baby named David. I loved that baby and just knew he was mine and I was going to be the best big sister in the world. I would go upstairs to his room each morning, knock on the door, and say "Good morning, baby David!" He would look up at me and smile and my heart would absolutely melt. I was so proud of being his big sister!

One morning I ran up the stairs, knocked on his door and said, "Good morning, baby David," just as I had done every day for months since he was born. That morning was different. David did not look at me and smile. I felt in my five-year-old gut that something was wrong. I ran downstairs and said to my mother, "Mom, come quickly, baby David has turned a really pretty shade of blue." She immediately dropped the frying pan she was holding and ran upstairs with lightning speed. She knew what that meant, but I had no idea. She then sprinted next door to our pediatrician's house, and he came running over. The doctor tried to get baby David to start breathing again, but it was too late. Baby David had died in the middle of the night.

We now have a name for that medical condition called SIDS (sudden infant death syndrome). In those days, we just called it a broken heart and had no idea how or why baby David had died.

I remember at that moment, a strong lie came into my five-year-old mind that said, "You killed your baby brother." I did not come from a spiritual family and had no idea that in the Bible Jesus said, "The thief comes only to steal and kill and destroy; I have come that they may have life, and have it to the full." (John 10:10) The thief is the devil who tried to convince me that I had killed my baby brother. I lived with that secret fear, guilt and shame for 35 years until God showed me the truth.

I got married right out of college to David Mullarkey, my college cheerleading partner at Jacksonville University. He was the oldest of three boys. The middle brother, named Johnny, was my favorite new brother-in-law. He and I had very similar personalities: Both loved life, loved to have fun and loved other people. During Johnny's senior year in high school, he was voted, "MOST FUN," and he was just that.

After graduation from Wolfson High School, Johnny went to work at Florida Feed Mills. This mill loaded and unloaded train cars full of grain. He and his two best friends from high school all started working on the same day at Florida Feed Mills. All three of them were going to start college in the fall at Florida State University and wanted to save up enough money to have fun at college.

Johnny and one of his friends, Mitch Davis, arrived early for their first day of work. They were told by the supervisor to go clean out hopper car #3, but were given no instructions.

They found some brooms and climbed up the high ladder, attached to the train, to get into the train car where the grain was. Then they started sweeping the leftover grain into the middle of the metal plates that were hooked together on top of the train car.

When their third friend arrived to work on time that day, the same supervisor told him to go turn on hopper car #3. Not knowing his two best friends were inside the top of car #3, he did as instructed: He turned on the grain shoot. That shoot automatically opened up the metal plates that Johnny and Mitch were standing on. Neither Johnny nor Mitch could find anything to hold onto to prevent what was happening to them. As they floundered trying to stay on top of the grain, both boys were suddenly sucked under, into the train carload of grain. There was no way to escape being suffocated to death. It took emergency first responders two hours to empty the grain out of the train car before anyone was able to get to the two dead bodies of these new high school graduates. It was a tremendous tragedy for the entire city of Jacksonville. The funeral was the largest in the city's history, and unto this day, its size is unmatched.

Johnny's death brought back those same feelings I had when I was five years old. I was traumatized, yet once again, because of the death of a brother. I had no idea what happened to people after they died, because no one ever took the time to explain to me about eternal life. To help my hurting heart, I wrote many poems about Johnny's death, about a God I really did not know and the pain I was experiencing. I was so afraid that I would be the next to die. I had a deep sense of fear that I would not live past the age of 30.

Two years later when I was 26 years old, I was teaching at Episcopal High School, when I had a surprise visit from Joe Mullarkey, my father-in-law. I thought he was coming to watch me teach to see how well I was doing. Instead of coming into the classroom to observe my teaching, he asked me to please step outside the classroom door. After he shut the door, he put his hands on my shoulders and told me my older brother, Peter, had died in an automobile accident at Lake Lanier in Georgia. He was 28 years old. Once again, I had to face death. At the young age of 26, I had lost all three brothers and was now an only child. My brothers were the closest people to me in my life, other than my mother and husband. I never wanted to be an only child.

I was totally devastated and blamed God for allowing me to have to suffer, yet once again. I started to stop believing that there even was a God. After all, how could a good God allow me to suffer three deaths of my beloved brothers?

I formulated a plan to deal with my sorrow. I decided to bury the pain and never talk about death again or attend any more funerals. I did not even tell my friends that I had any brothers. I compartmentalized the pain to keep my sanity. It actually worked for almost 20 years.

Because I was traumatized, after the death of my three brothers, I never went to the cemetery to pay my respects. It would have been much too painful.

DYING IS
AN IMPORTANT
PART OF LIFE

hope now you can better understand why I had such a tremendous fear of death. After my mom had been in the nursing home for seven months, something happened one day. When Dad and I arrived, Mom was sitting in a wheelchair, still able to smile when she saw us. We knew she could not talk verbally, so we would communicate through body language.

When I walked out of the nursing home with my dad, I felt in my heart that my mother was going to die the next day. I knew God would be with me this time, and I hoped He would get me through this tremendously fearful thing called "death." I did not say anything to my dad about what I knew was going to happen the next day, because I was so shocked and extremely upset. I did not want to upset him as well.

After dropping off my father at his house, I went to the beach, my greatest place of refuge. I walked and talked to God and cried harder than ever before. I kept repeating these words, "God, I can't do this." I had closed off that part of my life 20 years ago and could not go back to that place. I even tried to make a deal with God praying, "Please do anything you want to me, but don't make me have to face death again. I can't do it!" After spending a couple of hours praying and crying out to God, I went back home very frightened and still very much upset.

The next day, I told my dad I would meet him at the nursing home so he could leave whenever he needed to go. I did not know what to expect. All I knew was Mom was going to die that day.

When I arrived, my mom was in a semi-coma lying in her bed. When my dad entered the room he said, "What's the matter with your mom? Why isn't she up having breakfast?" I shared with my dad that Mom was going to die that day, enter heaven and be with the Lord. Even though Dad was not a believer, he knew enough not to question what I was sharing with him. He paused and then said, "I can't do this." I said, "Dad, why don't I leave the room, you say your goodbyes to Mom and then drive home, and I will stay with her until she passes." He agreed and spent a little time with his wife of 60 years saying his goodbyes. Saying goodbye is always a very difficult thing to do, even when the person you are saying goodbye to does not recognize who you are. My dad thanked me and said he would be at home waiting to get my call after she passed away.

To say I was brave or ready for this moment would be a huge lie! I was scared speechless. I prayed, "God please get me through this and show me what I am supposed to do." As soon as I said "Amen" I felt a peace come over me and a thought to open her nightstand drawer, get the Bible out I had given to her, and look up all the scriptures about heaven.

As I read the scriptures about heaven, I was holding one of her hands. Her eyes were closed, and there was no motion in her body, but I sensed she could hear me. At one point, I said to her, "Mom, if you want me to stop reading I will." Immediately, she squeezed my hand and would not let it go. I knew she could hear me and understand what I was saying even though she was in a semi-coma. I realized my reading God's Word about heaven was comforting her. I was getting stronger as I read each passage. My favorite one was when Jesus said to His followers, *"Do not let your hearts be troubled. You believe in God; believe also in me. ² My Father's house has many rooms; if that were not so, would I have told you that I am going there to prepare a place for you? ³ And if I go and prepare a place for you, I will come back and take you to be with me that you also may be where I am. ⁴ You know the way to the place where I am going."* (John 14:1-4)

When I finished reading all the scriptures about heaven, I went out to the main dining room and found Mr. White. I went up to his wheelchair and asked if he would go with me to my mom's room. Mr. White had a severe case of Parkinson's disease and was wheelchair bound. His mind was still sharp though. I asked if he would come to my mother's room and sing to her. He was the leader of a church choir before getting Parkinson's disease and entering the nursing home. He agreed, so I wheeled him to Mom's room. When I arrive, there was a Catholic priest praying over my mother. We were not Catholic, but I was surely grateful for his prayers. Mr. White agreed to sing "Amazing Grace." While he was singing in his very broken voice, the priest, Mr. White and I were around Mom's bed, and I was holding her hand. As he finished "Amazing Grace," my mom stopped breathing and her spirit went to heaven. In the New Testament they call death "falling asleep" because when we ask Christ into our hearts we are given the gift of eternal life with Him. In John 3:16, Jesus said, *"For God so loved the world that he gave his one and only Son, that whoever believes in him shall not perish but have eternal life."*

I was amazed this death was so peaceful and easy for me to go through because God was with me every step of the way. I then I realized God had taken me through my greatest fear and delivered me from the trauma of losing my loved ones. He had intervened in an amazing way.

The greatest supernatural thing in my life happen the morning after my mother's death. I woke up and my body was flooded with the most powerful peace, love and joy I had ever experienced. As I laid in bed I prayed to God saying, "Oh God what is this that I am feeling?" The tremendous peace, love and joy that I was experiencing was exactly what my mother was feeling in heaven, and I would someday be with her experiencing that forever and ever. That deep peace, love and joy lasted 30 minutes. I knew at that moment I had nothing to fear and was reassured that death was an important part of life. The scripture I had never even read before came to me at that moment, *"Where, O death, is your victory? Where, O death, is your sting?"* (1 Corinthians 15:55) Jesus overcame death, and so did my mother. Her spirit is in heaven, and I will spend eternity with my best friend, who now has the mind of Christ who knows all things.

God has a wonderful way of taking each of us through the hardest times in our lives. He then uses those experiences to help others going through similar things in their lives. After the death of my mother, God gave me several people, who I had the honor of sitting with as they breathed their last breath and passed on to heaven. His words are so true when Paul said: *³ Praise be to the God and Father of our Lord Jesus Christ, the Father of compassion and the God of all comfort, ⁴ who comforts us in all our troubles, so that we can comfort those in any trouble with the comfort we ourselves receive from God.* (2 Corinthians 1:3-4)

FIGHTING THE
DISEASE

Studies have shown that there are quite a few things we can do to help fight dementia. Here are three ways we can start to see some improvement in our cognitive memories.

1. LIFESTYLE:
    A. Exercise: Get up and do something active. Studies reveal that being sedentary contributes to the problem of memory loss. Most people suffering with memory loss would rather sit or sleep and not be active. Budgeting time EVERY DAY to exercise will enhance brain activity. Set a goal to keep your brain healthy. Doing something is better than doing nothing. Walking at a good

pace is a great place to start. Increase your distance until you have reached your goal. Going to a gym and doing weight-bearing exercises will increase muscle mass and keep bones and joints healthier, which is especially important to help prevent falls. Endorphins are released, both during and after exercise, that help reduce depression. In addition, energy levels are increased both during and after exercise, which means the brain is working and our memory is improving.

B. Sleep: When we are asleep, we secrete growth hormones, the brain clears out debris, and our muscles relax to help repair our bodies. At 1:30 a.m. the most growth hormones are released. The ideal time to sleep for a healthy brain is seven hours and 30 minutes. Sleep apnea is dangerous because the body needs down time in order to be healthy. Get into a sleep routine. Before going to bed, shut down all electronic screens because the lights make our brain think it is daytime. Limit the amount of water after dinner. This way waking up in the middle of the night can lessen. Reading, while lying down in bed, helps the eyes and mind become sleepy and the body begins to relax.

2. CONDITIONING:

A. Diet: Stay away from processed foods. They tend to cause inflammation that attributes to memory loss. Eat healthy fruits and vegetables in place of starchy foods. Sugar is one of the worst things we can eat in relation to memory loss. Processed sugars are in packaged treats. Stevia and Truvia are plant-based sugars that are healthier than processed sugar. Natural honey and guava are wonderful substitutes for sugar as well.

The Alzheimer's Research Foundation has research and other articles on ways to help slow this disease, including diet:

Food and Brain Health

Healthy Foods	Foods to Avoid
• Whole grains	• Red meats
• Fresh fruits	• Butter
• Vegetables	• Margarine
• Fish	• Cheese
• Beans	• Fast foods
• Nuts	• Sweets
• Olive oil	• High-sodium foods

(Alzheimer's Research Foundation)

B. Outdoors: Going outdoors and being in the fresh air enhance brain health. Vitamins C & D are from the sun and are healthy for our bodies, minds and immune systems. Gardening and yard work have proven to increase healthy brain chemicals. In addition, fishing, swimming and boating are wonderful relaxers for our bodies and souls.

3. ENHANCEMENTS:

A. Supplements: They help in absorption problems. Vitamins, especially B-12, are highly recommended for memory enhancement. Dopamine depravation is the number one cause of vitamin B-12 deficiency. Dopamine can be increased by exercising regularly and by taking supplements.

B. Meditation and Prayer: help the mind, spirit and soul connection and the entire person becomes healthier. Research has shown that people who pray daily have higher levels of contentment and peace and better marriages and sex lives.

C. Yoga, Pilates, and Fitness: These trainings push the body beyond normal, which enhances brain activity.

D. Brain Stimulation Activities: Crossword puzzles, word scramble, etc. help keep our brains active. Reading research or other intellectual articles and journals, while taking notes, also helps your mind to become more alert. Learning a foreign language and learning a new musical instrument have proven to help increase brain activity.

E. Cognitive Exercises: These can include counting backwards from 100 by sevens; drawing three-dimensional objects; repeating three-five words and recalling them five minutes later; and generating as many words as possible that start with the same letter.

4. ATTITUDE: Practicing gratitude triggers the release of dopamine and serotonin in the brain, providing a quick mood boost. Repeating aloud the blessings you see happening in the life of the memory-impaired person, as well as the caregiver, helps set a positive mood. Looking at old pictures helps bring back happy memories and activates the brain. Telling funny stories and sharing jokes help people laugh, which releases endorphins that relieve stress. Playing music that is familiar to the memory-impaired sets an upbeat mood. Many people can remember the words to old songs even though they cannot remember much else. If at all possible, keep bad news away from the

person with memory issues. Bad news can cause depression and dismay. The national news media continually shows negative pictures that cause fear and anxiety.

All her life, my mom was loved by everyone who knew her. My teen friends always called her the "Greatest Mom" and would come by just to talk with her.

APPENDIX

I hope this book has been helpful to you. If it has, please share it with a friend or family member who is caring for someone with this disease. Together we can help each other by bringing laughter that can lighten our load.

A percentage of all sales will be donated to the Alzheimer's Research Foundation in hopes that a cure will be found shortly.

If you would like to share some of your stories with me, I would be honored to read them. You can contact me at Pam@projectsos.com or go to my website at www.drpamrobbins.com.

CPSIA information can be obtained
at www.ICGtesting.com
Printed in the USA
LVHW101626220422
716974LV00003B/53

9 781664 237193